*Prashna Upanishad
and Commentary*

By
Charles Johnston

Copyright © 2021 Lamp of Trismegistus. All rights reserved. No part of this publication may be reproduced or transmitted in any form or by any means, electronic or mechanical, including photocopying, recording, or by any information storage and retrieval system, without permission in writing from Lamp of Trismegistus. Reviewers may quote brief passages.

ISBN: 978-1-63118-494-9

*Esoteric Classics:
Eastern Studies*

Other Books in this Series and Related Titles

Isha Upanishad and Commentary by Charles Johnston (978-1-63118-490-1)

Kena Upanishad and Commentary by Charles Johnston (978-1-63118-491-8)

Katha Upanishad and Commentary by Charles Johnston (978-1-63118-493-2)

Mundaka Upanishad and Commentary by Charles Johnston (978-1-63118-496-3)

Mandukya Upanishad and Commentary by Charles Johnston (978-1-63118-497-0)

Atma Bodha & Tattva Bodha by Adi Shankara &c (978-1-63118-401-7)

The Crest-Jewel of Wisdom by Adi Shankara (978-1-63118-475-8)

Catholicism, Yoga and Hinduism by Hartmann &c (978-1-63118-478-9)

Yoga, Hatha-Yoga and Raja-Yoga by Annie Besant (978-1-63118-476-5)

The Tree of Wisdom by Nagarjuna (978-1-63118-470-3)

The Path of Light: A Manual of Maha-Yana Buddhism (978-1-63118-471-0)

Buddhist Psalms by Shinran (978-1-63118-465-9)

Tao Te Ching & Commentary by Lao Tzu & C Johnston (978-1-63118-495-6)

The Sepher Yetzirah and the Qabalah by M P Hall (978-1-63118-481-9)

The Hymns of Hermes by G. R. S. Mead (978-1-63118-405-5)

The Golden Verses of Pythagoras: Five Translations (978-1-63118-479-6)

Gnosis of the Mind by G. R. S. Mead (978-1-63118-408-6)

The Hymn of Jesus by G. R. S. Mead (978-1-63118-492-5)

The Book of the Watchers by Enoch (978-1-63118-416-1)

The Secrets of Enoch by Enoch (978-1-63118-449-9)

The Gospel of the Nativity of Mary by St. Matthew (978-1-63118-448-2)

Audio versions are also available on Audible, Amazon and Apple

Table of Contents

Introduction...7

Prashna Upanishad
Translated by Charles Johnston...9

A Vedic Master
Commentary on the Prashna Upanishad
By Charles Johnston...23

Prasna Upanishad
Translated by Swami Nikhilananda...45

INTRODUCTION

The word "esoteric" can be difficult to define. Esotericism in general can be seen less as a system of beliefs and more as a category, which encompasses numerous, different systems of beliefs. It's a bit of juxtaposition, since the word "esoteric" indicates something that few people know about, while the term itself broadly covers numerous philosophies, practices, areas of study and belief systems.

In a greater sense, Esotericism acts as a storehouse for secret knowledge, which is often considered ancient (*by tradition, if not by fact),* passed down from generation to generation, in private. At various times in history, simply possessing the knowledge of some of these subjects, was considered illegal and a jailable offence, if discovered. This usually included such general topics as Alchemy, Pharmacology, Qabalah, Hermeticism, Occultism, Ceremonial Magic, Astrology, Divination, Rosicrucianism and so on. Collectively, these areas of study were often referred to as the esoteric sciences.

Sometimes, the outer garment of a subject isn't esoteric, while what is hidden beneath it, is. As an example, Freemasonry isn't necessarily esoteric by nature (at *least not anymore),* but certain signs, passwords and handshakes given to the candidate during their initiation, are in fact, esoteric, in the sense that they are hidden from the general public.

Today, in the twenty-first century, such topics are readily available at bookstores across the country, and numerous mainsteam publishers offer beginners guides and coffee-table volumes on many of these subjects, intended for mass appeal. Books like *"The Secret"* have turned previously arcane topics into household knowledge. All that being the case, however, it isn't to say that there still aren't buried secrets to uncover, ancient wisdom being ignored and forgotten mysteries to be explored. In fact, it is often that we are only able to further our own studies by standing on the shoulders of these disappearing giants.

Lamp of Trismegistus is doing its part to help preserve humanity's esoteric history by making some of these classics available to those students who are seeking to unearth the knowledge of these ancient colossi.

So, be sure to check other titles from our *Esoteric Classics* series, as well as our *Occult Fiction*, *Theosophical Classics*, *Eastern Studies*, *Foundations of Freemasonry Series*, *Supernatural Fiction*, *Paranormal Research Series*, *Studies in Buddhism* and our *Christian Apocrypha Series*. You can also download the audio versions of most of these titles from Amazon, Apple or Audible, for learning on the go.

PRASHNA UPANISHAD

Translated by Charles Johnston

Sukeshan son of Bharadvaja, Satyakama son of Shiva, Gargya grandson of Surya, Kaushalya son of Ashvala, Bhargava of Vidarbha, Kabandhin son of Katya: these, verily, devoted to the Eternal, set firm in the Eternal, seeking after the supreme Eternal, drew near to the Master Pippalada, with kindling-wood in their hands, saying, He will declare it all.

To them, verily, the Seer said, Dwell together with me for a year more, with fervour, service of the Eternal and faith; then ask questions according to your desire. If we know, we shall declare everything to you.

And so Kabandhin son of Katya approaching asked:

Master, whence, verily do these beings come forth in birth?

To him he said:

The Lord of beings was desirous of offspring. He brooded with fervour. Brooding with fervour, he produces a pair, Matter and Life. These two will make beings manifold for me, said he.

The sun, verily, is Life, and Matter, the moon; Matter, verily, is everything here, the formed and the unformed; therefore form, verily, is Matter.

And so the sun, rising, enters the eastern space; thereby it gathers up the eastern lives among its rays. As it illumines the southern, the western, the northern, the lower, the upper, the intermediate spaces, as it illumines all, thereby it gathers up all the lives among its rays.

Thus, verily, the Fire-lord, the universal, all-formed Life arises.

> It is this that is declared in the Vedic verse:
> The all-formed, the golden, the all-knowing,
> The final goal, the one light, fervent.
> Thousand-rayed, hundredfold turning,
> The Life of beings, rises this sun.

The circling year, verily, is a Lord of beings. Of it there are two courses, the southern and the northern. Therefore they who worship, saying, "Offerings and rewards are our work!" win for themselves the lunar world. They, verily, return again. Therefore those seers who desire offspring follow the southern course. Matter, verily, is this Path of the Fathers.

And so by the northern, by fervour, by service of the Eternal, by faith, by wisdom seeking the Divine Self, they win the sun. This is the home of lives, this is the immortal, the fearless, this is the higher way; from this, they return not again. This is the resting place. And so there is this verse:

The five-footed father, twelve-faced, they declare,
In the upper half of heaven, a giver of sustenance.
But these others call him the far-shining one in the upper heaven,
Set in a seven-wheeled chariot of six spokes.

The month, verily, is a Lord of beings. Its dark half is Matter, and the bright, Life. Therefore these seers offer sacrifice in the bright half, but the others, in the other.

Day and night, verily, is a Lord of beings. Of this, verily, day is Life, and night is Matter. They waste their life who find love in the outward, but service of the Eternal finds love in the hidden.

Food, verily, is a Lord of beings. From it, verily, is the seed of life, from which these beings are born forth. Therefore they who fulfil the vow of the Lord of beings, produce a pair.

Theirs, verily is the world of the Eternal,
Whose are fervour and service of the Eternal,
In whom truth is set firm.

Theirs is the stainless world of the Eternal; not theirs, in whom are crookedness, untruth, or glamour.

And so Bhargava of Vidarbha asked him:

Master, how many bright powers uphold a being? How many cause this to shine forth? Which of them is the chiefest?

To him he said:

Radiant ether is a bright power, air, fire, water, earth; voice, mind, sight and hearing also. They, shining forth , declare, We uphold this frame, establishing it. To them the chiefest Life said: Fall not into delusion. I, verily, dividing myself fivefold, uphold this frame, establishing it.

They were incredulous. He, from pride, ascends as it were above. As he departs upward, the lesser lives all, verily, depart; and as he returns, all, verily, return. Like as the bees all follow the honeymakers' king when he departs, and all return when he returns, so did voice, mind, sight and hearing. They, rejoicing, praise the Life:

This burns as the Fire-lord, this is the sun,
This is the Rain-lord, this the Wind-lord,
This is the Earth, Matter, the bright one,
Being, non-being and what is immortal.
As the spokes in the nave of a wheel,
In the Life all is established;
Verses and formulas and chants,
Sacrifice and weapon and prayer.
As Lord of beings thou movest in the germ,

Thou, verily, art born forth;
To thee, Life, these beings bring the offering,
Thou, who standest firm through the lives.
Thou art chief bringer of offerings to the bright powers,
Of the Fathers, thou art the first oblation;
Thou art righteousness and truth of seers,
Of the line of Atharvan and Angiras.
Thou art Indra, Life, by thy radiance,
Thou art Rudra the preserver;
Thou movest in the sky as the sun,
Thou art the Master of the stars.
When thou descendest as rain,
These thy beings, Life,
Stand rejoicing, for they say,
We shall have food according to our desire.
Thou art the Exile, Life, the one Seer,
Thou art the consumer, the good Lord of all;
We are the givers of thy food,
Thou art our Father, the great Breath.
That form of thine which dwells in speech,
That form of thine in hearing and sight,
That which is spread forth in mind,
Make it auspicious! Go not forth!
All this is under Life's sway,
Whatever is set firm in the three heavens;
Guard us as a mother her sons,
Grant us grace and understanding!

    And so Kaushalya son of Ashvala asked him:

Master, whence is this Life born? How does it come into this body? Or dividing itself, how is it established? Through what does it depart? How does it lay hold of what is outside? How is it with reference to the Self?

To him he said:

Many questions thou askest! Thou art bent on the Eternal, therefore I tell it to thee.

From the Divine Self, verily, this Life is born. As the shadow extended beside a man, so is it with this. Through the power of mind it comes into this body.

Like as a king, verily, enjoins his lords, saying, Rule over these villages and these villages! thus, verily, the Life disposes hither and thither the lesser lives: in the lower powers, the downward-life; in sight, in hearing, in the mouth and nostrils, as the forward-life it establishes itself; but in the midst, the binding-life, for this binds together the food which has been offered, and from this these seven flames arise.

In the heart is the Self. Here are the hundred and one channels; from each of these, a hundred; from each of these, two and seventy thousand branch channels. In these, the distributing-life moves.

And by one, the upward-life ascends; it leads through holiness to a holy world, through evil to an evil world, through both to the world of men.

As the sun, verily, the Life rises outwardly, and it links itself with this forward life in the power of sight; and the power that is in earth, supports the downward-life; what is between, the shining ether, is the binding-life; the wind is the distributing-life.

The radiance is the upward-life. Therefore, when his radiance has become quiescent, he goes to rebirth through the powers dwelling in mind.

According to his thinking, he comes to life; his life being linked by the radiance with the Self, leads him to the world that he has moulded for himself.

Whosoever, thus knowing, knows the Life, his offspring fails not; he becomes immortal. There is this verse:

He who knows the origin, the entrance, the dwelling and the lordship of Life fivefold, he reaches the immortal; knowing this, he reaches the immortal.

And so Gargya, grandson of Surya, asked him:

Master, in the man here, which powers sleep, and which wake in him? Which is the bright one who beholds dreams? Whose is this happiness? In what are all these bright powers set firm?

To him he said:

As, Gargya, the rays of the sun going to his setting all become one in his radiant circle, and again, when he rises again, they go forth, thus, verily, all this becomes one in the higher bright power, Mind. Because of this then the man hears not, sees not, smells not, tastes not, speaks not, handles not, enjoys not, puts not forth, walks not; he sleeps, they say.

The life-fires, verily, wake in this dwelling; the household fire, verily, is the downward-life; the sacrificial fire is the distributing-life; because it is brought forward from the household fire, from being brought forward, the fire of oblation is the forward-life. The binding-life is so called because it binds together the up-breathing and the down-breathing, the two oblations. Mind, verily, is the sacrificer. The fruit of the sacrifice is the upward-life. Day by day it brings the sacrificer to the Eternal. Here this bright power in dream experiences greatness; what was seen, as seen he beholds again; what was heard, he hears again, verily, as an object heard; what has been experienced by the different powers in their regions, he again perceives according to each power, the seen and unseen, the heard and unheard, the experienced and unexperienced, the real and unreal; all he perceives, as the All he perceives.

When he is enveloped by the radiance, the bright power then beholds no dreams; and so then in this body that happiness arises. As, dear, the birds come home to the tree to rest, so, verily, all this comes to rest in the Higher Self: earth and forms of earth, water and forms of water, fire and forms of fire, air and forms of air, radiant ether and forms of radiant ether, sight and what is to be seen, hearing and what is to be heard, the power of smell and what is to be smelled, taste and what is to be tasted, touch and what is to be touched, voice and what is to be spoken, the two hands and what is to be handled, the formative power and what is to be formed, the power which puts forth and what is to be put forth, the two feet and the power of going, the mind and what is to be thought, the intelligence and what is to be understood, self-reference and what is referred to self, imagination and what can be imagined, the radiance and what can be illumined, the life-breath and what can be supported.

For it is he who sees, touches, hears, smells, tastes, thinks, understands, acts, the Self of understanding, the spiritual man; he is set firm in the higher, imperishable Self.

He reaches the higher imperishable, who, verily, knows that shadowless, bodiless, colourless, radiant, imperishable; he, dear, knowing all, becomes All. And there is this verse:

The Self of understanding with all the bright powers,
All lives and beings are set firm in this;
He, dear, who knows this imperishable,
He, knowing all, has entered the All.

And so Satyakama, son of Shiva, asked him:

Master, he who among the sons of men should meditate on Om until his life's end, which of the worlds does he thereby win?

To him he said:

Om, Satyakama, is the higher and lower Eternal. Therefore he who knows, resting in this, comes to one of these worlds.

If he meditate on one measure, thereby illumined he quickly returns to this world. The Rig verses lead him to the world of men; there endowed with fervour, service of the Eternal, faith, he experiences greatness.

And so if he be possessed of two measures in his mind, he is led by the Yajur verses to the mid-world, the lunar world. Having enjoyed expansion in the lunar world he returns again.

Again, he who meditates on this Om with three measures, and, through this Om, on the higher spiritual man, enveloped in the radiance, in the sun, like as a serpent is released from its slough, so is he released from the darkness of sin; he is led up by the Sama verses to the world of the Eternal; he perceives the Spiritual Man, who is above the highest assembly of lives. As to this, there are these verses:

The three measures, subject to death, are united, joined together, not disunited.

When the outer, inner and middle are perfectly joined together in acts of meditation, the knower is not shaken.

By the Rig to this world, by the Yajur to the mid-world, by the Sama to the world the seers know; to that world, resting in Om, goes he who knows, to that which is full of peace, ageless, immortal, fearless.

And so Sukeshan, son of Bharadvaja, asked him:

Master, Hiranyanabha of the Koshalas, the Rajput, coming to me, asked me this question: Son of Bharadvaja, knowest thou the Man of sixteen parts? I said to the prince, I know him not; if I knew him, how should I not tell him to thee? He dries up, root and all, who speaks untruth, therefore I deign not to speak untruth. Ascending his chariot in silence, he departed. I ask thee this:

Where is that Man?

To him he said:

Here, verily, within the body, dear, is the Man in whom the sixteen parts are manifested.

He, beholding, thought: In what going forth shall I go forth? Or in what set firm shall I be set firm?

He put forth the Life; from the Life, faith, ether, air, fire, the waters, the earth, the powers, mind, food, also came forth; from food, valour, fervour, the sacred verses, works, the worlds; and name also in the worlds.

As these rolling rivers, flowing oceanward, reaching the ocean, find there their setting; their name and form are lost and they are called ocean; so of this seer, the sixteen parts, moving toward the Spiritual Man, on reaching the Spiritual Man, find their setting; their name and form are lost and they are called the Spiritual Man: so he becomes partless, immortal. As to this, there is this verse:

In whom the parts are set firm, like the spokes in the wheel's nave, him I know as the Spiritual Man to be known, therefore let not death perturb you.

To them he said:

Thus far know I this supreme Eternal; there is naught beyond.

Praising him, they said:

Thou art our father, who hast caused us to cross over to unwisdom's further shore. Obeisance to the supreme Seers! Obeisance to the supreme Seers!

A VEDIC MASTER

Commentary on the
PRASHNA Upanishad

Translated from the Sanskrit with an Interpretation
By Charles Johnston

Prashna Upanishad, "the Mystical Teaching of the Questions," brief though it be, is a masterly summary of the Secret Wisdom. It illustrates two fundamental principles in the method of the Eastern Schools: first, that the seekers for wisdom must be tried and tested by a protracted period of probation, during which they must show that they possess real aspiration, selfless devotion and moral purity; second, that the disciple is taught in response to his own questions. He must have worked out the question for himself, and it must be a real question, before he is given the answer.

The six questions here asked and answered are not taken at random. They begin with the universal, and proceed gradually to the particular, so that both macrocosm and microcosm are covered. And, without pressing the likeness too far, we may see, in this group of six disciples under their Master, a symbol of the six principles of man's complex nature, synthesized by the seventh, Atma, the Divine Self.

Sukeshan son of Bharadvaja, Satyakama son of Shiva, Gargya grandson of Surya, Kaushalya son of Ashvala,

Bhargava of Vidarbha, Kabandhin son of Katya: these, verily, devoted to the Eternal, set firm in the Eternal, seeking after the supreme Eternal, drew near to the Master Pippalada, with kindling-wood in their hands, saying, He will declare it all.

To them, verily, the Seer said, Dwell together with me for a year more, with fervour, service of the Eternal and faith; then ask questions according to your desire. If we know, we shall declare everything to you.

And so Kabandhin son of Katya approaching asked:

Master, whence, verily do these beings come forth in birth?

To him he said:

The Lord of beings was desirous of offspring. He brooded with fervour. Brooding with fervour, he produces a pair, Matter and Life. These two will make beings manifold for me, said he.

The sun, verily, is Life, and Matter, the moon; Matter, verily, is everything here, the formed and the unformed; therefore form, verily, is Matter.

And so the sun, rising, enters the eastern space; thereby it gathers up the eastern lives among its rays. As it illumines the southern, the western, the northern, the lower, the upper, the intermediate spaces, as it illumines all, thereby it gathers up all the lives among its rays.

Thus, verily, the Fire-lord, the universal, all-formed Life arises.

It is this that is declared in the Vedic verse:

The all-formed, the golden, the all-knowing,
The final goal, the one light, fervent.
Thousand-rayed, hundredfold turning,
The Life of beings, rises this sun.

The circling year, verily, is a Lord of beings. Of it there are two courses, the southern and the northern. Therefore they who worship, saying, "Offerings and rewards are our work!" win for themselves the lunar world. They, verily, return again. Therefore those seers who desire offspring follow the southern course. Matter, verily, is this Path of the Fathers.

And so by the northern, by fervour, by service of the Eternal, by faith, by wisdom seeking the Divine Self, they win the sun. This is the home of lives, this is the immortal, the fearless, this is the higher way; from this, they return not again. This is the resting place. And so there is this verse:

The five-footed father, twelve-faced, they declare,
In the upper half of heaven, a giver of sustenance.
But these others call him the far-shining one in the upper heaven,
Set in a seven-wheeled chariot of six spokes.

The month, verily, is a Lord of beings. Its dark half is Matter, and the bright, Life. Therefore these seers offer sacrifice in the bright half, but the others, in the other.

Day and night, verily, is a Lord of beings. Of this, verily, day is Life, and night is Matter. They waste their life who find love in the outward, but service of the Eternal finds love in the hidden.

Food, verily, is a Lord of beings. From it, verily, is the seed of life, from which these beings are born forth. Therefore they who fulfil the vow of the Lord of beings, produce a pair.

*Theirs, verily is the world of the Eternal,
Whose are fervour and service of the Eternal,
In whom truth is set firm.*

Theirs is the stainless world of the Eternal; not theirs, in whom are crookedness, untruth, or glamour.

The answer of the Master Pippalada begins with the First Logos: the triune Being, manifested threefold, as the Lord of beings, the Life, and Matter, or primordial substance. The general tendency of the whole answer is, by applying the law of correspondence, to show that this threefold division is found throughout the whole of the manifested worlds, here represented by the sun and moon, the circling year, day and night, food. The unfolding of the whole cosmic process is implied.

The cosmic process is first illustrated by the visible sun and moon, the sun shining by its own light, the moon reflecting that light; the two thus symbolizing Spirit and Matter.

But every phrase should be carefully thought out; every epithet is full of meaning. For example, the sevenfold division of the spaces, east, south, west, north, lower, upper, intermediate, corresponds to every sevenfold system, such as the Sevenfold Heavenly Host, the seven globes, the seven races. It may be said that the globes or the races develop in succession as the life-power of the Logos enters them and penetrates them with its rays. The Vedic verse, on the surface a description of the visible sun, is likewise a parable of the spiritual sun, the Logos.

What is said of the circling year has also its deeper meaning. It refers to the two ways, Liberation and Reincarnation; also called the Path of the sun and the Path of the moon, or the Path of the Gods and the Path of the Fathers.

And there is here also an allusion to the fundamental division in the spiritual history of India: on the one side, the Mystery teaching of the Rajputs; on the other, the sacrificial system and priestcraft of the Brahman hierarchy, who say, "Offerings and rewards are our work!" As against this sacrificial system, the Rajput sages taught "fervour, service of the Eternal, faith, wisdom, the seeking of the Divine Self." This is the way of the Gods, of the sun, of Liberation; those who go that way return not again. They are not constrained by Karma to fall again into rebirth.

In later ages, Krishna and Siddhartha the Buddha taught this way of the sun; both were Rajputs and not Brahmans; both pointed out the way of Liberation.

The five-footed father is the year divided into five seasons: the cold season, the hot season, the lesser rains, the greater rains, the period after the rains. The twelve faces are the twelve months. The seven-wheeled chariot is the sevenfold body of the sun: the visible sun with its higher principles. The wheel with six spokes set in the nave is a symbol of every system of six principles synthesized by the seventh.

The contrasted halves of the year, and of the months, are elsewhere used in the Upanishads to symbolize the positive and negative poles of a series of ascending planes; the soul which passes from the smoke of the funeral pyre, through the negative pole of plane after plane, is the soul following the way of reincarnation under the bondage of Karma. The soul which rises from the flame of the funeral pyre to the positive pole of each plane is the soul free from the bondage of Karma, following the path of Liberation.

It is said that theirs is the world of the Eternal, whose are fervour and service of the Eternal. This latter also has the technical meaning of chastity, as opposed to the desire of offspring. The graces which lead to the Eternal are those already enumerated, as possessed by the six disciples who came to the Master Pippalada. They came, bringing kindling-wood in their hands: the readiness to be enkindled, to "take fire."

And so Bhargava of Vidarbha asked him:

Master, how many bright powers uphold a being? How many cause this to shine forth? Which of them is the chiefest?

To him he said:

Radiant ether is a bright power, air, fire, water, earth; voice, mind, sight and hearing also. They, shining forth, declare, We uphold this frame, establishing it.

To them the chiefest Life said: Fall not into delusion. I, verily, dividing myself fivefold, uphold this frame, establishing it.

They were incredulous. He, from pride, ascends as it were above. As he departs upward, the lesser lives all, verily, depart; and as he returns, all, verily, return. Like as the bees all follow the honeymakers' king when he departs, and all return when he returns, so did voice, mind, sight and hearing. They, rejoicing, praise the Life:

This burns as the Fire-lord, this is the sun,
This is the Rain-lord, this the Wind-lord,
This is the Earth, Matter, the bright one,
Being, non-being and what is immortal.
As the spokes in the nave of a wheel,
In the Life all is established;
Verses and formulas and chants,
Sacrifice and weapon and prayer.
As Lord of beings thou movest in the germ,
Thou, verily, art born forth;
To thee, Life, these beings bring the offering,

Thou, who standest firm through the lives.
Thou art chief bringer of offerings to the bright powers,
Of the Fathers, thou art the first oblation;
Thou art righteousness and truth of seers,
Of the line of Atharvan and Angiras.
Thou art Indra, Life, by thy radiance,
Thou art Rudra the preserver;
Thou movest in the sky as the sun,
Thou art the Master of the stars.
When thou descendest as rain,
These thy beings, Life,
Stand rejoicing, for they say,
We shall have food according to our desire.
Thou art the Exile, Life, the one Seer,
Thou art the consumer, the good Lord of all;
We are the givers of thy food,
Thou art our Father, the great Breath.
That form of thine which dwells in speech,
That form of thine in hearing and sight,
That which is spread forth in mind,
Make it auspicious! Go not forth!
All this is under Life's sway,
Whatever is set firm in the three heavens;
Guard us as a mother her sons,
Grant us grace and understanding!

The second question and answer carry us from the universal to the individual, to what we may call an enumeration of the Seven Principles. These are Atma, the Life, and the five elements: radiant ether, air, fire, water, earth; with the powers, through the Logos, "the Lord of beings." There is also an outline of the twin doctrines of liberation and reincarnation. The second answer sketches what we are accustomed to call the Seven Principles, both of the worlds and of man; the inferior principles being but aspects and manifestations of the one Divine Principle. In the third answer, the teaching of the Principles is further developed through their correspondence with the life-forces of the body, which are manifestations of the one Life.

The fourth question and answer, translated above, lead to the consideration of the planes of consciousness which are treated more fully in the answer to the fifth question.

The disciple asks concerning sleep. The Master answers, going back for his guiding thought to the first teaching, the manifestation of the worlds and man through the out-breathing of the Logos. As there is an out-breathing, so there is also an in-drawing. For the worlds, this in-drawing comes at the end of the world-period; for man, it comes at death, as has already been told in the second answer. But there is also sleep, the sister of death, in which the same in-drawing takes place, though it is an in-drawing of consciousness and not of substance. The body is not dissolved as in death, but sinks into a torpor, awaiting the return of the powers on awaking. The body thus resting, with its powers indrawn, is likened to the house with its sacrificial fires; and the process of going to sleep is compared to a sacrifice, whose reward is the upward tide of aspiration, which carries the consciousness upward toward spiritual life.

But the mid-world must first be passed through, the realm of dreams. We are told that the scenery of the dream-world is made up of the images of things seen and heard and diversely perceived in the realm of waking. These images are reflected from below. But there are also reflections from above, images of things not seen nor heard in the world of waking; spiritual images which should lead the consciousness upward to the living, spiritual world; images of beauty, truth and goodness, reflections of immortal Beauty, Truth and Goodness. That living, spiritual world is the dwelling of the Higher Self, the Immortal, which has put forth Mind and the bright powers into the manifested world as its servants, to do its bidding and reap its harvests.

And just as sleep is, in a sense, a rehearsal of death, so this ascension of the consciousness in sleep is a foreshadowing of the final ascent of consciousness in the great Liberation, which is the true theme of all Mystery teachings.

And so Satyakama, son of Shiva, asked him:

Master, he who among the sons of men should meditate on Om until his life's end, which of the worlds does he thereby win?

To him he said:

Om, Satyakama, is the higher and lower Eternal. Therefore he who knows, resting in this, comes to one of these worlds.

If he meditate on one measure, thereby illumined he quickly returns to this world. The Rig verses lead him to the world of men; there endowed with fervour, service of the Eternal, faith, he experiences greatness.

And so if he be possessed of two measures in his mind, he is led by the Yajur verses to the mid-world, the lunar world. Having enjoyed expansion in the lunar world he returns again.

Again, he who meditates on this Om with three measures, and, through this Om, on the higher spiritual man, enveloped in the radiance, in the sun, like as a serpent is released from its slough, so is he released from the darkness of sin; he is led up by the Sama verses to the world of the Eternal; he perceives the Spiritual Man, who is above the highest assembly of lives. As to this, there are these verses:

The three measures, subject to death, are united, joined together, not disunited.

When the outer, inner and middle are perfectly joined together in acts of meditation, the knower is not shaken.

By the Rig to this world, by the Yajur to the mid-world, by the Sama to the world the seers know; to that world, resting in Om, goes he who knows, to that which is full of peace, ageless, immortal, fearless.

The syllable Om is made up of three measures: a-u-m. These are taken to represent the three states of consciousness, physical, psychical, spiritual; united together, as Om, they represent the divine consciousness. As a secondary symbolism, the three Vedas, the Rig, Yajur and Sama Vedas, are taken, likewise standing for the three states of consciousness; the Veda, as a unity, standing for the divine consciousness.

Consciousness limited to the physical is represented by the first measure of Om; since there is no subjective life in such a case, nothing to build the scenery of the paradise between death and rebirth, such a one is reborn forthwith.

The added subjective, but not yet spiritual, consciousness, is represented by the second measure of Om. At death, such a one goes to the "lunar" paradise, so called because it shines by reflected light and, after waxing, will wane again.

Spiritual consciousness is represented by the third measure of Om. The radiance is the Principle called Buddhi; the sun is the Logos. Through the illumination of Buddhi, he is united with the Logos, this union being Liberation. The Logos, whom Shankaracharya calls "the First-born," is the Spiritual Man, above the highest assembly of lives.

It is the teaching of the Upanishads that man in sleep enters the spiritual consciousness, but that, passing downward again through the mid-world, the world of dreams, he loses all remembrance of that consciousness; so far as his outer knowledge is concerned, spiritual consciousness comes to an end when the man returns to waking consciousness. Therefore all three, physical, psychical and spiritual consciousness, have their ending for him; they are "subject to death." But they are perfectly united through meditation, through spiritual illumination; the spiritual man, dwelling in spiritual consciousness, uses psychical and physical consciousness for the purposes of his work, while standing unshaken in the spiritual world. This is the ageless, immortal, fearless world, his everlasting home.

And so Sukeshan, son of Bharadvaja, asked him:

Master, Hiranyanabha of the Koshalas, the Rajput, coming to me, asked me this question: Son of Bharadvaja, knowest thou the Man of sixteen parts? I said to the prince, I know him not; if I knew him, how should I not tell him to thee? He dries up, root and all, who speaks untruth, therefore I deign not to speak untruth. Ascending his chariot in silence, he departed. I ask thee this: Where is that Man?

To him he said:

Here, verily, within the body, dear, is the Man in whom the sixteen parts are manifested.

He, beholding, thought: In what going forth shall I go forth? Or in what set firm shall I be set firm?

He put forth the Life; from the Life, faith, ether, air, fire, the waters, the earth, the powers, mind, food, also came forth; from food, valour, fervour, the sacred verses, works, the worlds; and name also in the worlds.

As these rolling rivers, flowing oceanward, reaching the ocean, find there their setting; their name and form are lost and they are called ocean; so of this seer, the sixteen parts, moving toward the Spiritual Man, on reaching the Spiritual Man, find their setting; their name and form are lost and they are called the Spiritual Man: so he becomes partless, immortal. As to this, there is this verse:

In whom the parts are set firm, like the spokes in the wheel's nave, him I know as the Spiritual Man to be known, therefore let not death perturb you.

To them he said:

Thus far know I this supreme Eternal; there is naught beyond.

Praising him, they said:

Thou art our father, who hast caused us to cross over to unwisdom's further shore. Obeisance to the supreme Seers! Obeisance to the supreme Seers!

Fully understood, the Spiritual Man concerning whom the question is put appears to be the Logos; the "sixteen parts" include, or represent, the seven worlds, the seven principles, and the activities of the principles in the worlds.

The essence of the answer is the return to the Logos, through the great Liberation; as the rivers which, rising as clouds, have come forth from the ocean, return once more to the ocean when their cycle is fulfilled, so, when their time is fulfilled, all beings return to the Logos, becoming that from which of old they came forth; becoming again the partless Immortal.

PRASNA UPANISHAD

Translated by Swami Nikhilananda

First Praśna

Question I

1

OM. Sukeśā, the son of Bharadvāja, and Satyakāma, the son of Śibi, and Sauryāyani, belonging to the family of Garga, and Kausalya, the son of Aśvala, and Vaidarbhi, belonging to the family of Bhrigu, and Kabandhi, the son of Katya—all these, devoted to Brahman and firm in Brahman, and seeking the Supreme Brahman, approached, fuel in hand, the venerable Pippalāda with the thought that he would tell them everything about Brahman.

2

The rishi said to them: Stay with me a year more, practising austerities, chastity, and faith. Then you may ask questions according to your desire. If we know we shall tell you all.

3

Then Kabandhi, the son of Katya, came to him and asked: Sir, whence are these creatures [including human beings of all castes and classes] born?

4

To him the teacher said: Prajāpati, the Creator, was desirous of progeny. He performed austerities, and having performed austerities, created the pair, the moon (rayi) and the sun (prāna). He said to Himself: "These two should produce creatures for Me in manifold ways."

5

The sun is, indeed, prāna, life; the moon is rayi, food. Food is, indeed, all this—what has form and what is formless. Therefore everything having form is, indeed, food.

6

Now the sun, when it rises, enters the eastern quarter and thereby enfolds the living beings of the east in its rays. And when it illuminates the southern, the western, the northern, the lower, the upper, and the intermediate quarters—when it illuminates everything—it thus enfolds all living beings in its rays.

7-8

That sun rises every day—the sun, which is the soul of all creatures, the soul of all forms, which is life and fire. This has been described by the following rik:

[The wise know him who] is in all forms, full of rays, all-knowing, non-dual, the support of all life, the eye of all beings, the giver of heat. There rises the sun, the thousand-rayed, existing in a hundred forms, the life of all creatures.

9

The year, verily, is Prajāpati, and there are two paths thereof: the Southern and the Northern. Those who perform sacrifices and engage in pious actions, as duties to be done, win only the World of the Moon; verily they return hither again. Therefore the rishis who desire offspring travel by the Southern Path. This Path of the Fathers is rayi, food.

10

But those who seek the Self through austerity, chastity, faith, and knowledge travel by the Northern Path and win the Sun. The Sun, verily, is the support of all lives. He is immortal and fearless; He is the final goal. Thence they do not return. This path is blocked [for the ignorant]. Concerning it there is the following verse:

11

Some call Him the father with five feet and with twelve forms, the giver of rain, and the dweller in the region above the sky. Others, again, say that the world is fixed in the omniscient Sun, endowed with seven wheels and six spokes.

12

The month, verily, is Prajāpati. Its dark half, verily, is food, rayi; its bright half, the eater, prāna. Therefore some rishis perform sacrifice in the bright half, some in the other half.

13

Day and night, verily, are Prajāpati. Of these, day is the eater, prāna, and night, the food, rayi. Those who join in sexual enjoyment by day verily dissipate life; but to join in sexual enjoyment by night is, verily, chastity [for the householder].

14

Food, verily, is Prajāpati. From that comes semen; from semen are all these creatures born.

15

Those, therefore, who practise this rule of Prajāpati beget a pair. But Brahmaloka belongs to those who observe austerity and chastity and in whom truth is firmly established.

16

The stainless World of Brahmā belongs to those in whom there is no crookedness, no falsehood, no deception.

Second Praśna

Question II

1

Then Vaidarbhi, belonging to the family of Bhrigu, asked him: Sir, how many gods support the body of the created being? How many of these manifest their power through it? And which one, furthermore, is paramount?

2

To the disciple he said: Space, ākāśa, verily is that god—the wind, fire, water, earth, speech, mind, eye, and ear, as well. These, having manifested their glory, said boastfully: "We [each of us] support this body and uphold it."

3

To them prāṇa, the chiefmost said: "Do not fall into delusion. I alone, dividing myself into five parts, support this body and uphold it." But they were incredulous.

4

Prāṇa, out of pride, rose upward, as it were, from the body. Now, when it rose upward all the others rose upward also, and when it settled down they all settled down with it. As bees go out when their queen goes out and return when she returns, even so did speech, mind, eye, and ear. They, being satisfied, praised prāna.

5

It burns as fire, it is the sun, it is the rain; it is Indra, it is the wind, it is the earth, it is food. It is the luminous god. It is being and non-being; it is immortality.

6

As spokes in the hub of a wheel, all are fixed in prāna, including the Rig-Veda, the Yajur-Veda, the Sama-Veda, the kshattriyas, and the brāhmins.

7

As Prajāpati thou movest about in the womb; it is thou, indeed, who art born again. To thee, O Prāna, creatures bring offerings, to thee who dwellest in the body with the organs.

8

Thou art the chief bearer of oblations to the gods and the first offering to the departed fathers; thou art the true activities of the rishis, of the Atharvāngiras.

9

Indra thou art, O Prāna, and Rudra, too, in prowess. Thou art the Protector. Thou movest in the sky; thou art the sun, the lord of lights.

10

When, O prāna, thou showerest down rain, these creatures of thine are delighted, thinking there will be as much food as they desire.

11

Thou art vrātya, O Prāna, and the Ekarshi Fire that devours the butter. Thou art the Supreme Lord of all. We are the givers of the butter that thou consumest, O Mātariśva! Thou art our father.

12

That form of thine which abides in speech, which abides in the ear, which abides in the eye, and which pervades the mind, make propitious. Go not away!

13

All that exists here is under the control of prāna, and also what exists in heaven. Protect us as a mother her sons; bestow upon us prosperity and wisdom.

Third Praśna

Question III

1

Then Kausalya, the son of Aśvala, asked Pippalāda: Sir, whence is this prāna born? How does it come into this body? How does it abide in the body after it has divided itself? How does it depart? How does it support the external and how the internal?

2

To him the teacher replied: You are asking difficult questions; you must be exceedingly devoted to Brahman. Therefore I will answer you.

3

This prāna is born of Ātman. As a shadow is cast by a person, so this prāna is, by Ātman. Through the activity of the mind it comes into this body.

4

As an emperor commands his officials, saying: "Rule these villages or those," so this prāna employs the other prānas, each in its separate place.

5

Prāna engages apāna in the organs of excretion and generation; he himself moves through the mouth and nose and dwells in the eye and ear. In the middle is samāna; it distributes equally what has been offered as food [in the fire in the stomach]. From this prāna fire arise the seven flames.

6

The ātman dwells in the heart, where there are one hundred and one arteries (nāḍi); for each of these there are one hundred branches, and for each of these branches, again, there are seventy-two thousand subsidiary vessels. Vyāna moves in these.

7

And then udāna, ascending upward through one of them, conducts the departing soul to the virtuous world, for its virtuous deeds; to the sinful world, for its sinful deeds; and to the world of men, for both.

8

The sun, verily, is the external prāna; for it rises, favouring the prāna in the eye. The deity that exists in the earth controls the apāna of man. The space, ākāśa, between heaven and earth is samāna. The air is vyāna.

9

Fire, verily, is udāna; therefore he whose fire has been extinguished goes out for rebirth, with the senses absorbed in the mind.

10

Whatever one's thinking [at the time of death], with that one enters into prāna. Prāna joined with fire, together with the soul, leads to whatever world has been fashioned by thought.

11

The wise man who thus knows prāna does not lose his offspring and becomes immortal. As to this there is the following verse:

12

He who knows the origin of prāna, its entry, its place, its fivefold distribution, its internal aspect and also its external, obtains immortality; yea, he obtains immortality.

Fourth Praśna

Question IV

1

Next Sauryāyani, belonging to the family of Garga, asked: Sir, what are they that sleep in man, and what are they that remain awake in him? Which deity is it that sees dreams? Whose is the happiness [of deep sleep]? In whom, again, are all these gathered together?

2

To him Pippalāda replied: O Gārgya, as the rays of the sun, when it sets, are gathered in that luminous orb, and again go forth when it rises, even so, verily, all these—the objects and the senses—become one in the superior god, the mind. Therefore at that time a man hears not, sees not, smells not, tastes not, touches not, speaks not, grasps not, enjoys not, emits not, and does not move about. He sleeps—that is what people say.

3

The prāna fires remain awake in this city. Apāna is the Gārhapatya Fire, and vyāna, the Anvahāryapachana Fire. And prāna is the Āhavaniya Fire, so called from *being taken*—since it is taken from the Gārhapatya Fire.

4

Samāna is so called because it distributes *equally* the two oblations, namely, the out-breathing and the in-breathing; it is the priest. The mind, verily, is the sacrificer. Udāna is the fruit of the sacrifice, because it leads the sacrificer every day, in deep sleep, to Brahman.

5

There, in dreams, that god, the mind, experiences glory. Whatever has been seen he sees again; whatever has been heard he hears again; whatever has been experienced in different countries and quarters, he experiences again. Whatever has been seen or not seen, heard or not heard, and whatever is real or not real—he sees it all. He sees all, himself being all.

6

When the jiva is overcome by light he sees no dreams; at that time, in this body, arises this happiness.

7-8

As a bird goes to a tree to roost, even so, O friend, all this rests in the Supreme Ātman:

Earth and its subtle counterpart, water and its subtle counterpart, fire and its subtle counterpart, air and its subtle counterpart, ākāśa and its subtle counterpart, the eye and what can be seen, the ear and what can be heard, the nose and what can be smelt, the taste (tongue) and what can be tasted, the skin and what can be touched, the organ of speech and what can be spoken, the hands and what can be grasped, the organ of generation and what can be enjoyed, the organ of excretion and what can be excreted, the feet and what is their destination, the mind (manas) and what can be thought, the intellect (buddhi) and what can be comprehended, the ego (ahamkāra) and the object of egoism, the memory (chitta) and its object, knowledge (tejah) and its object, prāna and what is to be supported.

9

He, verily, it is who sees, feels, hears, smells, tastes, thinks, and knows. He is the doer, the intelligent self, the purusha. He is established in the Highest, the imperishable Ātman.

10

He who knows that imperishable Being, bright, without shadow, without body, without colour, verily attains the Supreme, the undecaying Purusha. O my good friend, he who knows Ātman becomes all-knowing, becomes all. About it there is the following verse:

11

He, O friend, who knows that imperishable Being wherein rests the intelligent self, together with the gods, the prānas, and the elements—he becomes all-knowing and enters into all.

Fifth Praśna

Question V

1

Then Satyakāma, the son of Śibi, asked Pippalāda: Sir, if among men someone should here meditate on the syllable AUM until death, which world, verily, would he win thereby?

2

He replied: O Satyakāma, the syllable AUM is the Supreme Brahman and also the other Brahman. Therefore he who knows it attains, with its support, the one or the other.

3

If he meditates on one letter (mātrā), then, being enlightened by that alone, he quickly comes back to earth after death. The ṛik verses lead him to the world of men. By practising austerity, chastity, and faith he enjoys greatness.

4

If, again, he meditates on the second letter, he attains the mind and is led up by the yajur verses to the intermediate space, to the Plane of the Moon. Having enjoyed greatness in the Plane of the Moon, he returns hither again.

5

Again, he who meditates on the Highest Person through this syllable AUM consisting of three letters, becomes united with the effulgent sun. As a snake is freed from its skin, even so he is freed from sin.

6

The three letters of AUM [if employed separately] are mortal; but when joined together in meditation on the total Reality and used properly on the activities of the external, internal, and intermediate states, the knower trembles not.

7

The wise man, meditating on AUM, attains this world by means of the rik verses; the intermediate world by means of the yajur verses; and that which is known to the seers by means of the sama verses. And also through the syllable AUM he realizes that which is tranquil, free from decay, death, and fear, and which is the Highest.

Sixth Praśna

Question VI

1

Then Sukeśā, the son of Bharadvāja, said to Pippalāda: Sir, Hiraṇyābha, the prince of Kosala, once came to me and asked this question: "O son of Bharadvāja, do you know the Person with sixteen parts?" I said to the prince: "I do not know Him; if I knew Him, why should I not tell you? Surely he who speaks what is not true withers away to the very root; therefore I should not speak untruth." Then he silently mounted his chariot and went away. Now I ask you: Where does that Person dwell?

2

Pippalāda said to him: That Person—He from whom these sixteen parts arise—is verily here within the body.

3

The Purusha reflected: "What is it by whose departure I shall depart, and by whose staying I shall stay?"

4

He created prāna; from prāna faith, space, air, fire, water, earth, the organs, mind, food; from food virility, austerity, the Vedic hymns, sacrifice, the worlds; and in the worlds He created names.

5

As these flowing rivers, bound for the ocean, disappear into the ocean after having reached it, their names and forms being destroyed, and are called simply the ocean—even so, these sixteen parts of the seer, whose goal is the Purusha, disappear into the Purusha after having reached Him, their names and forms being destroyed, and are called simply the Purusha. He becomes free of parts and immortal.

On this there is the following verse:

6

Know Him, the Purusha, who alone is to be known and in whom the parts rest firm, like the spokes in the nave of a wheel, that death may not affect you.

7

Pippalāda said to them: Thus far, indeed, I know the Supreme Brahman; there is nothing higher than this.

8

And they, worshipping him, said: Thou, indeed, art our father—thou who hast taken us across our ignorance to the other shore. Adoration to the supreme rishis! Adoration to the supreme rishis!

www.ingramcontent.com/pod-product-compliance
Lightning Source LLC
LaVergne TN
LVHW041458070426
835507LV00009B/674